At a Glance Series — DVD and Lesson Book

DVD Beginning Bass

Written by Joe Charupakorn and Chad Johnson

Video Performer: Gio Benedetti

ISBN: 978-1-4584-8517-5

HAL•LEONARD® CORPORATION

7777 W. BLUEMOUND RD. P.O. BOX 13819 MILWAUKEE, WI 53213

TABLE OF CONTENTS

Introduction

Welcome to *DVD Beginning Bass*, from Hal Leonard's exciting new At a Glance series. Not as in-depth and slow moving as traditional method books, the material in *DVD Beginning Bass* is presented in a snappy and fun manner and will help you get some great bass lines under your fingers in virtually no time at all. Plus, the At a Glance series uses real musical examples by real artists to illustrate how the concepts you're learning are used by the masters. For example, in *DVD Beginning Bass*, you'll learn bass lines from classics like The Beatles' "Eight Days a Week," Van Halen's "You Really Got Me," and Nirvana's "Come As You Are," to name just a few.

Additionally, each book in the At a Glance series comes with a DVD containing video lessons that correspond to the printed material. The DVD that accompanies this book contains four video lessons, each approximately 8 to 10 minutes in length, that correspond to the topics covered in *DVD Beginning Bass*. In these videos, ace instructor Gio Benedetti will get you started by first showing you in great detail the mechanics of how the bass works and how to hold the instrument. You'll then get a primer on reading, but unlike typical method books, you won't be reading through lame songs like "Mary Had a Little Lamb." Instead, you'll be working with bass lines from real songs right away. Additionally, you'll also learn some basic right-hand techniques and some beginning grooves to get you on the road to coming up with your own bass lines. As you work through *DVD Beginning Bass*, try to play the examples first on your own and then check out the DVD for additional help or to see if you played it correctly. As the saying goes, "A picture is worth a thousand words," so be sure to use this invaluable tool on your quest to learning bass guitar.

FIRST BASS LESSON

Congratulations on your choice to play bass. It's an awesome instrument that'll provide years of enjoyment, and you can feel good about the fact that you're one of the biggest supporting roles in any band situation. Before we start laying it down, we need to get familiar with all the parts of our instrument.

Bass Parts

The main part of the bass is called the **body**. Attached to it is the **neck**. At the end of the neck is the **headstock**, which contains the **tuners** and **tuning pegs**. The strings make initial contact at two points—the **nut** and the **bridge**.

The metal strips are called **frets**, which we use to play different pitches on each string. The dots on the fretboard are called **inlays** or **fret markers**, and they help us keep our place on the neck. When you use a strap, it attaches to the **strap buttons**.

On most electric basses, the **pickups** are mounted in the **pickguard**. The **knobs** control the volume and tone, and the **output jack** is where you plug in the instrument cord. The other end of the cord is plugged into the **amplifier**, which is what we use to rattle the walls.

Playing Position

Ok, now that you're familiar with the parts, let's talk about how to play. When seated, most people prefer to rest the bass on their right leg.

Rest your right forearm on the top of the body, as seen in the DVD. This can help to angle the neck slightly upward, which will assist with fretting. (If you're left-handed, obviously, these directions would be reversed.)

When standing, you attach your strap across the strap buttons and put your neck and your right arm through. Once you're sure the strap is secured, stand up. You can adjust the height of your strap so that the bass is at roughly the same place whether you're standing or sitting.

Tuning

Once you're in the proper position, it's time to get in tune. The four strings of the bass are tuned to the following pitches: E, A, D, and G.

We use the tuners, which loosen or tighten the strings, to tune each string. When you're tuning to a pitch, it's best to start from below and tune up to it. The string will remain more stable that way.

When you're starting out, sometimes it can be hard to hear whether you are perfectly in tune. In many cases, it's easiest to use an **electronic tuner** to tune with. A tuner can tell you whether a pitch is sharp, which means too high, or flat, which means too low.

To use the tuner, you plug the cord from your bass into the tuner and pluck a string. If the tuner tells you you're flat, or too low, then slowly tighten the tuner. Just turn it a little at a time, repluck the string, and watch the tuner's needle indicator move accordingly. Don't turn too much at once, because you might break a string if you go too high. Once the string is in tune, you just repeat the same thing for the other three strings.

Eventually, you'll want to learn to tune by ear. There are plenty of online resources that'll show you how to do this, and it gets easier with practice. After tuning by ear, you can check with the tuner to see if you got it right.

If you don't have an electronic tuner, you can try to match your notes to the ones played on the DVD.

Right-Hand Technique

Ok, now that you're in tune, let's get to some playing. Bass can be played with a *pick* or *fingerstyle*.

Pick Style
When using a pick, which is most common in rock styles, hold it between your thumb and first finger with the pointed end showing. Most people use a wrist motion when picking the strings.

Fingerstyle
When playing fingerstyle, which is common in all styles, the thumb usually rests on the pickup when we're playing on the thickest string.

Try plucking with your first finger on the thickest string a few times. Allow your finger to roll over the string smoothly. You don't want to pull up or out when plucking the string. That results in a thinner tone, and it's not as efficient.

When we play any other string, our thumb will move down and lightly touch the thickest string to keep it from ringing. Also notice that the plucking finger follows through and come to rest on the next string.

Alternating Fingers
Most players will alternate between their first and second fingers when playing at moderate or faster tempos, so it's a good habit to get into it early on. Once you get comfortable with this technique, you'll be able to play faster bass lines with less effort.

First try slowly alternating between your first and second fingers on the thickest string, the low E string. Use a smooth motion and don't claw at the strings. Let the amplifier do the work for you.

Generally speaking, a pick gets a more aggressive sound, whereas fingers get a mellower tone. It's recommended that you get well acquainted with both approaches so you'll be a more versatile player. You have a good deal of control with either method depending on where along the string you pluck.

If you pluck near the bridge, you'll get a brighter sound. Plucking near the neck gets a darker, warmer tone.

Fretting Technique

Ok, let's take a look at the left hand. When we play notes on the fretboard, it's called **fretting**. When fretting a note, place your thumb mid-way along the back of the neck and place your finger slightly behind the metal fret to produce the clearest sound.

 For practice, put your first finger just behind fret 3 on the low E string. When fretting a note, you only need to press the string down hard enough in order to get a good solid tone. If you don't press hard enough, the note will buzz or not ring out properly. On the other hand, pushing really hard is just unnecessary. In fact, you could make the note sound out of tune if you press too hard.

Experiment with trying to find just the right amount of pressure needed for a clear sound. Repeatedly pluck the string and increase the fretting pressure until you get a nice solid tone.

 Now, try using your second finger to play fret 4 on the low E string. Remember to push down just behind the fret.

Now move on to fret 5 using your pinky. Because the frets are so far apart down here on the neck, we usually play a two-fret spread like this with our first finger and pinky, to make it more comfortable to grasp. When fretting with your pinky, allow the other fingers to remain on the string behind it.

First Groove

 We'll finish off this lesson by learning our first little bass groove. This one sounds great and shouldn't be too hard. Watch the DVD first, and then we'll break down at the phrase note by note.

We're playing all the notes on the low E string. We start off by plucking that string open twice, and then we play fret 3 with our first finger, followed by fret 5 with our pinky. We repeat those four notes two more times. To finish it off, we play fret 3 again, holding it twice as long as the notes in the first part. And then hold the open E for twice as long as well.

At first, you can pluck each note with your first finger if you'd like, but once you get the hang of it, try alternating your fingers and speeding it up a little bit. Make it a goal to get an even sound from both plucking fingers. You don't want the notes played by one finger to unintentionally come out louder than the other.

Well that wraps it up for this lesson. Good luck in your musical endeavors, and remember: the bottom is where it's at!

MUSIC READING BASICS FOR THE BASS GUITAR

As many musicians have demonstrated in the past, learning to read music is not a pre-requisite to success. However, it's a huge advantage—especially if you're looking to get into studio work—and if you ask most successful non-reading musicians, they'll usually say they wish they could.

In this lesson, we'll learn the basics of music reading on the bass guitar. One of the advantages of learning to read music is that it's applicable to any instrument.

Reading Pitch

There are two elements of music notation—*pitch* and *rhythm*. Pitch indicates the highness or lowness of the note, and rhythm tells you how long or short you play (or don't play) each note. We'll start with pitch first.

The Staff

Traditional music notation is written of a *staff*, which consists of five parallel lines and four spaces between the lines. Notes are written on the lines, spaces, or sometimes both simultaneously (when playing more than one note at a time).

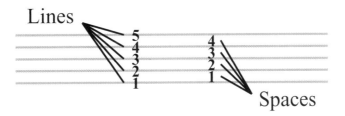

The Bass Clef

Pitches are represented vertically, moving from low to high on the staff. Since the ranges of instruments can vary so drastically—that is, a piccolo plays in a much higher range than a bass—we have ways of customizing this staff to suit different instruments.

This is done by the use of a *clef*. A clef lets you know which notes are assigned to which lines and spaces. As bassists, we read *bass clef*. When a bass clef appears on the staff, the notes of the lines, from low to high, are G, B, D, F, and A. Many players remember this with various phrases, such as "Good Boys Do Fine Always."

The notes of the spaces, from low to high, are A, C, E, and G. To easily remember this you can use the mnemonic "All Cows Eat Grass."

Musical Alphabet: A–B–C–D–E–F–G

Notice that, when moving from the lowest line up to the highest line, the notes progress up through the musical alphabet, which contains only seven letters: A through G. When G is reached, we start over again with A.

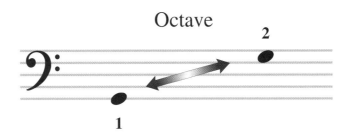

OCTAVE

The word for the same note name in a different register is octave. For example, we'd say that the G note on the bottom line is an octave lower than the one in the top space. Or we could say the top G note is an octave higher than the low one.

Ledger Lines

If you know the notes of the open strings, you know that the lowest string is an E note. But the lowest line on our staff is a G note. This is where *ledger lines* come into play. To extend the staff in either direction, we draw temporary ledger lines, which continue the same series of pitches above or below the staff. Our low E string is notated on the first ledger line below the staff.

Also be aware that the staff is not intended to coincide with the strings on the bass, as it does with tablature, which we'll explore shortly. The fact that the note in the highest space in the staff is "G" has nothing to do with the fact that the highest open string is G. It's just a coincidence, so don't read too much into it.

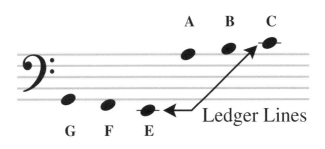

Reading Rhythm

Now let's take a look at the other aspect of music notation: the *rhythm*, which lets you know how fast to play the notes and for how long to hold them.

Here's a breakdown of the most common rhythms:

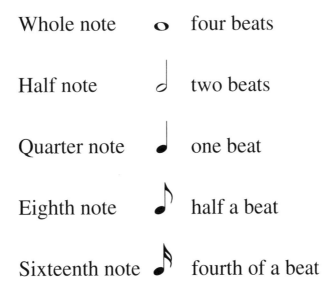

Whole note	𝅝	four beats
Half note	𝅗𝅥	two beats
Quarter note	♩	one beat
Eighth note	♪	half a beat
Sixteenth note	𝅘𝅥𝅯	fourth of a beat

Notice that each rhythmic division is half the length of the previous.

Measures (Bars)

In order to help keep our place, music is divided into *measures*, or *bars*, the same way text is divided into sentences. This makes it a lot easier to keep track of where you are.

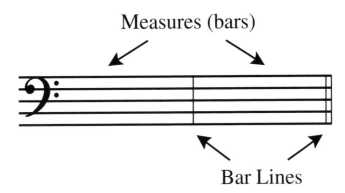

Measures (bars)

Bar Lines

Each measure will contain a certain amount of beats, which can vary depending on the song. By far, the most common amount is four beats per measure.

Time Signature

A *time signature* lets you know how many beats are in each measure, and how the beats are counted. It appears after the clef at the beginning of a piece of music and consists of two numbers—the top number tells you how many beats are in each measure, and the bottom number tells you what type of note is counted as one beat.

The most common time signature, 4/4, tells you that there are four notes per measure (indicated by the top 4), and the quarter note, which is indicated by the bottom 4 (a quarter is ¼), gets the beat.

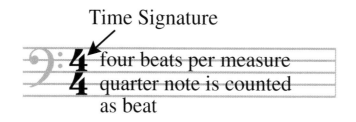

Exercises

Let's check out a few basic exercises to get some practice. We'll only be playing our open E string here, but there will be different rhythms used.

 Listen and follow along the first time with the DVD; then rewind and try to play along. Can you hear and feel how the different rhythms sound?

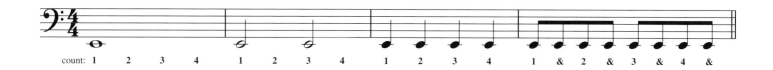

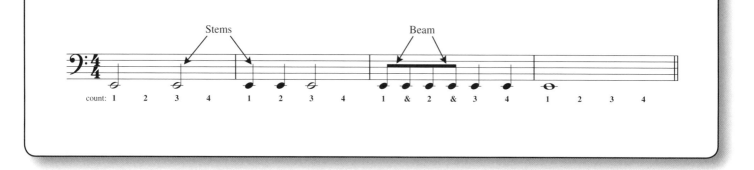

Rests

Just as we have different symbols for different note rhythms, we have different symbols for different lengths of silence, which are called *rests*. A rest is shown in the music any time you are supposed to not play anything.

Whole rest	▬	four beats
Half rest	▬	two beats
Quarter rest	𝄽	one beat
Eighth rest	𝄾	half a beat
Sixteenth rest	𝄿	fourth of a beat

Here's an exercise that mixes in rests. Simply touch the E string to mute it for the rests. This one is tricky so first watch the DVD. If you're still getting stuck after a few times, you might want to write in the beat numbers so you know where everything falls. Then count out loud as you play and also keep counting as you rest. Even when you're not playing, the beat is still moving on.

Combining Pitch and Rhythm

Now let's try adding in some other pitches besides our E string. If you don't know the names of the notes on your bass fretboard, you can find that information at numerous online resources. But here's a chart of the notes up through fret 5 on each string for now. You can copy this down if you'd like and memorize it later.

You'll notice that some notes have some funny-looking symbols next to them and two names. The symbols are called *accidentals*—sharps or flats. A *sharp* looks like ♯ and raises the pitch of a note by one fret. A flat looks like ♭ and lowers the pitch of a note by one fret. If a note has an accidental, the note can have two different names—a sharp version and a flat version. The "right" name to use can vary depending on some technical, theory-based reasons, but don't worry about that for now. As long as you can get to the right note, that is more important in the beginning.

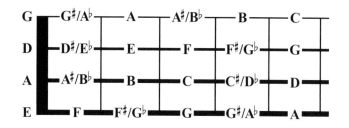

 This exercise will use three notes: E, G, and A. The E and G will be played on string 4, and the A will be played as the open A string. Now we are starting to make music!

Tablature

 There's another type of music notation for bass and guitar, which is called *tablature*, or "tab" for short. This is much easier to read. It shouldn't take more than a few minutes to understand the concept, and once you do, it can open up a whole new world of possibilities for you.

TABLATURE

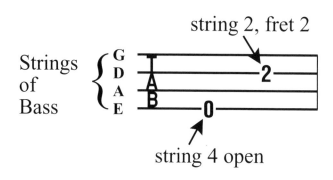

Bass tab consists of four horizontal lines—one for each string of the bass. The E, or fourth string, is on the bottom, and the G, or first string, is on top. Numbers appear on each line, telling you which fret to play—almost as easy as painting by numbers.

We'd read this line as follows:

Open E string, then fret 3 on the E string, then open A string, then fret 2 on the A string.

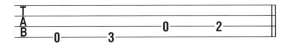

The main disadvantage of standard tab is that there's no indication of rhythm. Therefore, tab is often combined with standard notation. This not only tells you the notes and the rhythm, but the tab also specifies where exactly to play each note. (You can play most notes on the bass at several different spots on the fretboard.)

We can play this G note as the open G string, or at fret 5 on the D string, or at fret 10 on the A string, or even way up at fret 15 on the E string.

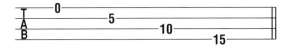

With tab, though, you'll know exactly where to play the notes. There are ways to indicate this positioning in standard notation as well, but it's mostly used in classical music.

Rhythm Tab

There's also a hybrid system called *rhythm tab*, which combines tab notes with rhythms. Check out how this standard notation can be converted to rhythm tab by employing stems and circles in the tab.

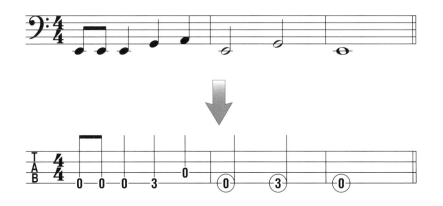

Let's start reading rhythm tab with Tom Petty's "Into the Great Wide Open." This one should be fairly easy. The "0" on the fourth string line means you pluck that string open—i.e., don't press any frets. The dots below the notes indicate *staccato*, which means you should play them short and clipped.

"INTO THE GREAT WIDE OPEN"
Tom Petty

Words and Music by Tom Petty
and Jeff Lynne

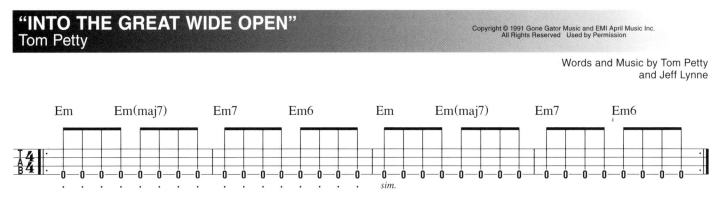

The intro riff to "Barracuda" is based primarily on the same open E string as "Into the Great Wide Open," but this one is played with a more upbeat rhythm. Compare both rhythm tab examples for a closer look—same notes for the most part, different rhythms.

"BARRACUDA"
Heart

Words and Music by Nancy Wilson,
Ann Wilson, Michael Derosier
and Roger Fisher

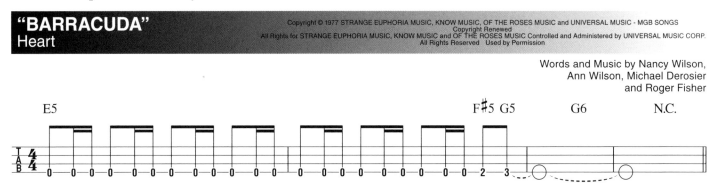

Let's move on from just the open string now. The intro to "Synchronicity II" uses the same rhythm as "Into the Great Wide Open," but it's played exclusively on string 4, fret 2.

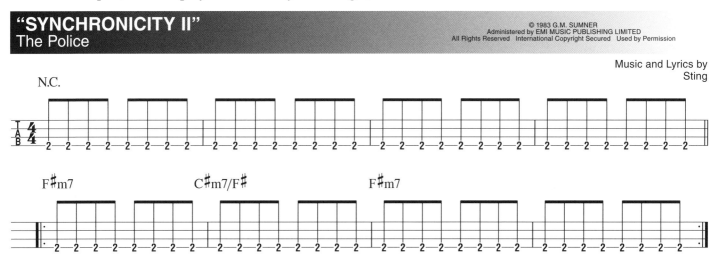

"SYNCHRONICITY II"
The Police

Music and Lyrics by
Sting

The intro to "I Can See for Miles" takes this same rhythmic idea but moves it to string 3, fret 7.

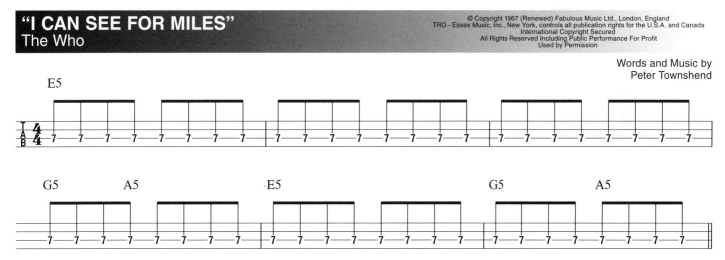

"I CAN SEE FOR MILES"
The Who

Words and Music by
Peter Townshend

Now let's try a riff that incorporates rests. The pauses in the intro to "Crazy Train" are what gives the bass figure its momentum and drive.

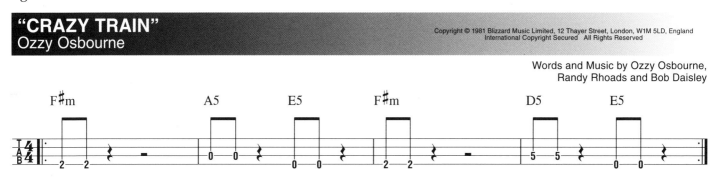

"CRAZY TRAIN"
Ozzy Osbourne

Words and Music by Ozzy Osbourne,
Randy Rhoads and Bob Daisley

Although rhythm tab does contain both rhythm and pitch, it's still incredibly beneficial to learn to read standard notation, as it will make you more well-rounded and allow you to exchange musical ideas with other instruments.

Well that's it for this lesson. There's still plenty to learn, but you've got a good foundation on which you can build a lifetime of musical knowledge. Enjoy!

RIGHT-HAND BASS TECHNIQUE

A solid right-hand technique plays a huge part in obtaining a nice, full tone on the bass and makes it possible to play more complex bass lines. That is why it's important to develop good habits early on. In this lesson, we'll look at the critical elements of the right-hand bass technique and how they factor into shaping your sound. We're going to look at two of the most essential techniques—fingerstyle and pick style.

Fingerstyle

Since it's a bit more ubiquitous in the bass world, we'll start with fingerstyle. Most players use their first and second fingers to pluck the strings. The thumb and third finger often come into play with muting, which we'll look at in a bit.

Basic Plucking Motion

Let's take a look at the basic plucking motion to get started. When we're plucking a note on the E string, our thumb usually rests on the pickup. Watch the DVD to see exactly how to rest your thumb.

Plucking the E String

Try to keep your wrist straight and place your first finger on the E string. When we pluck the string, we simply drag over it, allowing the finger to follow through. You don't want to pluck up and out from the body. Not only is that inefficient, but it results in a thinner tone that's usually not desirable.

If anything, we want to apply slight pressure in toward the body as we pluck. It doesn't take much though. It should be a very relaxed motion.

Now let's try the same thing with our second finger. It's important that you get equally comfortable with both fingers, because later on, you'll be using them both frequently.

Try using both fingers on the intro to "Dancing in the Street." Since the left hand doesn't have to fret any notes, you can concentrate solely on the right-hand plucking fingers.

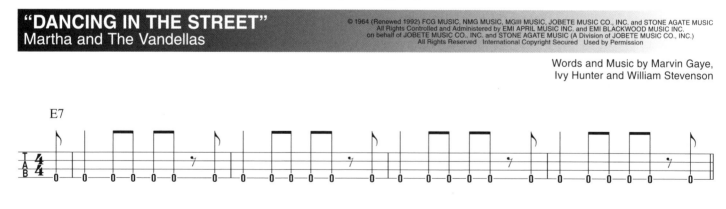

"DANCING IN THE STREET"
Martha and The Vandellas

Words and Music by Marvin Gaye,
Ivy Hunter and William Stevenson

Plucking the Other Strings

When we pluck any string besides the E, our thumb moves down and touches the E string to keep it quiet. Let's move to the A string.

Pluck the A string with your first finger, using the same motion as before, and allow the finger to follow through and come to rest on the E string. When plucking with the second finger, it's the same routine.

Now move to the D string and do the same thing, allowing the plucking finger to come to rest against the A string.

The first four measures of the intro to The Pretenders' "Brass in Pocket" alternates primarily between an open A string and fretted notes on the D string.

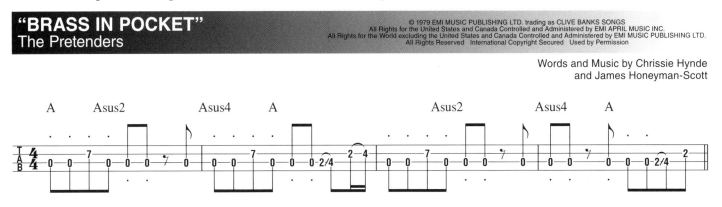

Muting Technique (Fingerstyle)

This brings us to an important topic—*muting*. Along with plucking the strings we want to sound, we also need to be concerned with quieting the ones we don't want to sound. An open string or two, ringing unintentionally, can create quite a messy sound.

When playing the E string, we don't have a problem, because the fret hand can keep the top three strings quiet. Watch the DVD to see the other strings being silenced with the fretting hand, as the low E string is plucked.

When we play the A string, our thumb mutes the E string. Also, our plucking finger follows through and rests on the E string, which mutes it as well. Technically, we don't even need our thumb on the low E to keep it quiet when playing the A string, but it's nice to have the extra safeguard in place to keep out unwanted noise.

When we play the D string though, things change. Watch the DVD to see what happens when we play the D string without touching the low E with our thumb. The E string will start to make some noise.

You hear how it starts to get muddy? This is why we have to mute lower strings that aren't being played. By bringing our thumb down to touch the low E, that will be kept quiet, and our plucking finger will follow through to rest on the A string, which will keep it quiet.

When we pluck the G string, however, we have a new problem. We can mute the E with our thumb, and our plucking finger will follow through to mute the D string, but now our A string is left open to ring out. There are two possible ways to deal with this.

Wandering Thumb

One method is called the "wandering thumb." With this method, the thumb would come down to touch the A string and also mute the E. Watch the DVD to see what that looks like.

Third Finger Mute

The other method is to involve the third finger of your plucking hand. When plucking the G string, you can touch the A string with your third finger to keep it quiet. Watch the DVD here as well.

Either method is effective, but one will probably feel more natural to you, so try both of them at first before you decide on one.

Muting Exercise

Now let's try an exercise to help master the muting technique. We'll play quarter notes on each string—two for each open string—moving up and down through them. With the combination of the fret-hand and pluck-hand muting, you should only hear one string ringing out at a time.

If you heard any two strings ringing out together, then isolate them and repeat the exercise until you've got it down. These little details are what will make you sound either like a polished pro or a struggling student.

Alternating Fingers

Now let's talk about *alternating fingers*. When we're playing lines that are a bit quicker, we alternate plucking between our first and second fingers. You may be able to get away with using only one finger at slower tempos, but when things start speeding up, alternating fingers is essential. It's best to get into the habit from the start.

 Let's say, for example, we're playing straight eighth notes on a string, which would sound like "1 and 2 and 3 and 4 and." Instead of using one finger to pluck each note, we'll switch back and forth with the two plucking fingers to make it easier. Compare how it feels to play the line using only one finger or with both, alternating. You should feel less tension in your plucking hand when you use two fingers.

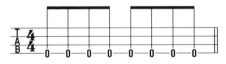

 Let's try it again, this time playing on the E string for one measure and then on the A string for the next. As you play through this, also strive to get each plucking finger to produce the same amount of volume so it sounds even and balanced. Continue working on this idea with the remaining strings as well. It's a crucial skill to develop early on.

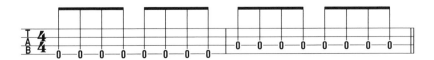

Freddie King's "Hide Away" makes use of mostly continual eighth notes. Practice alternating your fingers with this one.

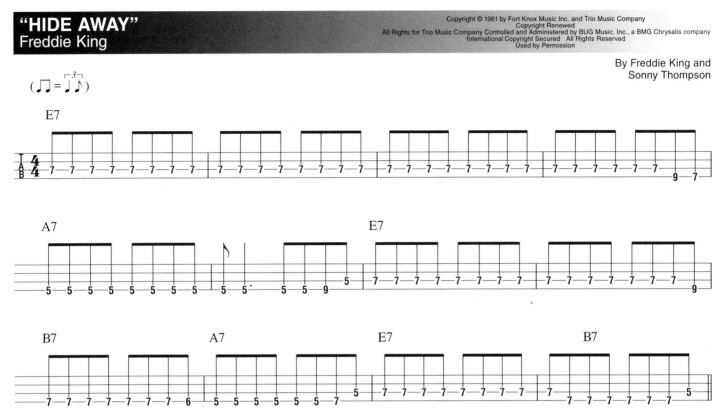

Crossing Strings: The "Raking" Technique

 Now we're going to talk about another extremely important technique called *raking*. We use this when we move down from one string to the next. When we say "down," we're talking about pitch—not geography. So another way to say it is moving from a thinner string to a thicker string—such as moving from the A string to the E string.

With the raking technique, we'll use one continuous plucking motion to handle both strings instead of alternating our fingers and plucking the A string with finger 1 and the E string with finger 2. Watch the DVD here to get a close-up look. We'll just drag, or rake, the same finger from the A string to the E in one smooth motion.

 This results in a smooth tone, and, again, is very efficient. When we're moving down through three or even all four strings, we use the same technique. Watch the DVD to see three- and four-string rakes.

 To help get this technique down, let's play an exercise that combines the rake technique with alternating fingers. The plucking fingers will be shown in the music, so be sure to follow them.

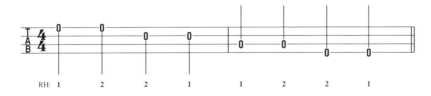

You can see that you're starting each string with a different finger. This may feel a little strange at first, but soon it'll become completely natural. Just start slowly at first and make sure you're getting a full sound even when raking into the lower (sounding) string.

ZZ Top's "Thunderbird" offers a great opportunity to practice the raking move. Although the bass line is primarily composed of a single C note pumping away in eighth notes, there are a few chances to practice the technique. For example, check out the rake into the E string from the A string in measure 4, and the rake into the D string from the G string in measure 6, among others.

"THUNDERBIRD"
ZZ Top

Words and Music by Billy F Gibbons,
Dusty Hill and Frank Beard

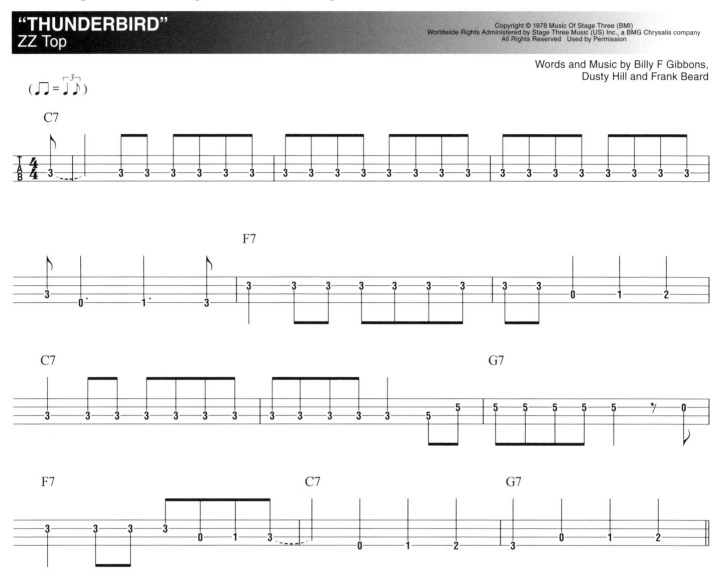

The Beatles' "Eight Days a Week" has a more active left-hand part, and every measure contains an opportunity to use the raking technique.

"EIGHT DAYS A WEEK"
The Beatles

Words and Music by John Lennon
and Paul McCartney

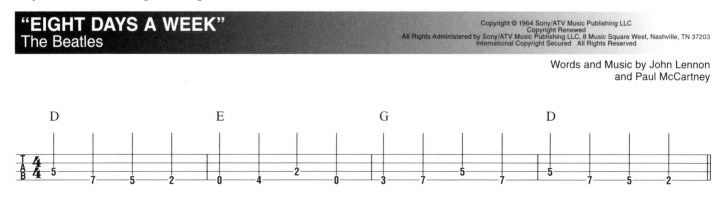

Pick Style

Let's talk a bit about playing with a pick now. This is most common in rock styles, but it occasionally shows up in others as well. The pick should be held between the thumb and first finger, with the pointed end showing. Most players use a wrist motion when plucking the string and angle the pick slightly downward so that it cuts through the string a little easier.

You'll notice that the pick style tone is quite different from fingerstyle. You get a little scraping sound using a pick, which is usually better-suited to more aggressive styles of music.

Muting Technique (Pick Style)

Earlier we talked about using muting open strings with a fingerstyle approach. When playing with a pick, we still need to mute unwanted strings from ringing out. This is achieved with our pick-hand palm.

When we're playing on the G string, our palm will be laying on the E, A, and D strings to keep them quiet. Watch the DVD to see what this looks like.

As we move down through strings, our palm moves down as well, muting only the strings below the one we're picking.

Palm Muting

A variation on this muting technique involves allowing the palm to also mute the string we're playing. This is sometimes called a *palm mute*.

When we do this, we want to make sure our palm touches the string just in front of the bridge. Just touch the string but don't apply pressure otherwise you'll only hear a muted sound without any of the note. If the mute happens too far out in front of the bridge, you won't really hear the pitch much at all.

The palm mute technique is a nice sound that can really fit the bill in some tunes. Paul McCartney used it to varying degrees on many Beatles songs.

Alternating Pick Strokes

As with alternating fingers in pick style, it's a good idea to become adept at alternating down- and up-strokes with the pick when you need to play faster lines.

Let's try a simple eighth-note line using alternate picking. Start with a downstroke, and then alternate every eighth note.

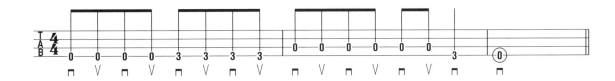

Use alternate picking for the intro to Judas Priest's "You've Got Another Thing Comin'." Since the left hand stays on the same note throughout, you can focus on your picking hand here.

"YOU'VE GOT ANOTHER THING COMIN'"
Judas Priest

Words and Music by Glenn Tipton,
Rob Halford and K.K. Downing

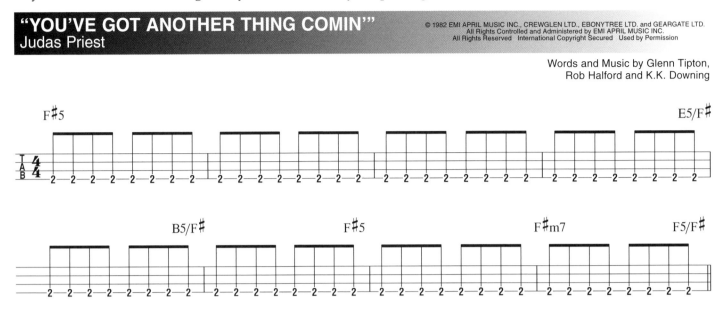

Well, that's gonna wrap it up for this lesson. Remember, it's much harder to unlearn a bad habit than it is to learn a good one from the beginning. So don't make it difficult on yourself. Put the work in now, and you'll be that much better off down the road. Enjoy!

FIRST BASS GROOVES

If you've got the basic playing technique down, and you know a few notes on the neck, you're ready to tackle some easy-but-great-sounding bass lines. Welcome to your first bass grooves.

Root Notes

Let's start with nothing but root notes. The root is the note that gives the chord its name. This means we'll be playing the root of the chord most likely played by a guitarist or keyboardist.

Here's a simple line in the key of G to start with.

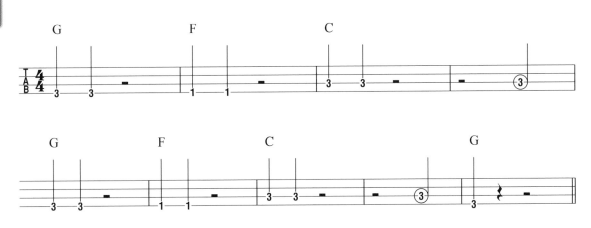

This simple example teaches us two things:

1. We don't need a lot of notes to create a groove; we used only three here.
2. What we don't play is sometimes just as important as what we do—that's an extremely important concept. The rests here are a large part of what makes it groove.

Even when a bass line is driving, sometimes keeping it simple and staying on the root produces the best bass lines. The bass line for "I Fought the Law" contains nothing but roots.

"I FOUGHT THE LAW"
Bobby Fuller Four

Words and Music by
Sonny Curtis

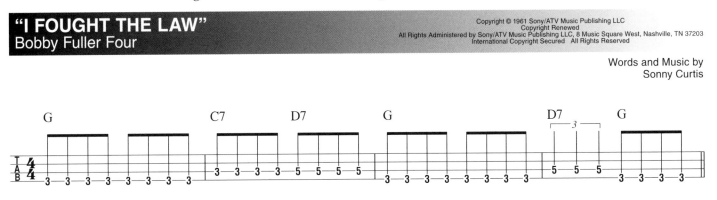

Approach Tones (or "Pushing")

Here's another groove that makes use of an *approach tone*, which is sometimes called a "push." The idea is to play a root in eighth notes but begin a half or whole step lower and "push" into it.

Since we're playing eighth notes, we'll alternate the plucking fingers as we talked about in the previous chapter. There are only two notes here—F# and G—but the F#, which is only used once per measure, played quickly as an eighth note, makes a big difference.

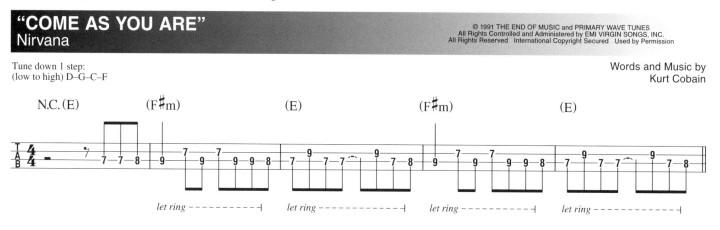

The initial "push" in "Come as You Are" gives the riff its forward motion.

"COME AS YOU ARE"
Nirvana

Words and Music by
Kurt Cobain

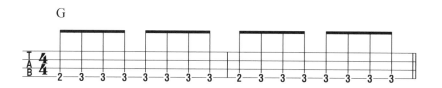

The quick chromatic "push" in "Another One Bites the Dust" is subtle but totally makes the line work.

"ANOTHER ONE BITES THE DUST"
Queen

Words and Music by
John Deacon

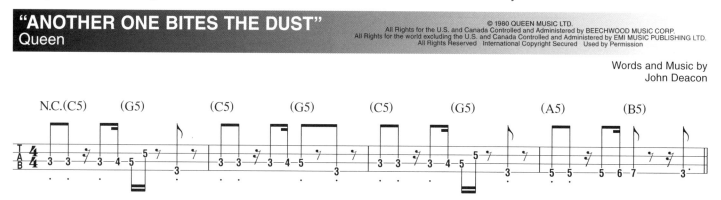

In the Beatles' "Lady Madonna," the fourth fret note on beat 4 of measures 1 and 3 connects fret 3 to 5, and gives the riff its signature drive.

"LADY MADONNA"
The Beatles

Words and Music by John Lennon
and Paul McCartney

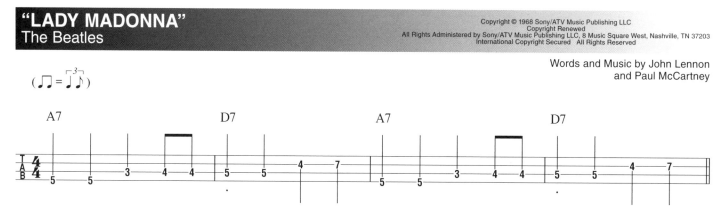

Rhythmic Hooks

Creating a *rhythmic hook* is another great way to groove. The notes can vary, but if you set up a nice repetitive rhythm, you can really sink into a nice groove. This line is almost all about the rhythm. It's in A minor with kind of an R&B style and uses a mix of playing and rests to give it that groove. As mentioned earlier, what you don't play is just as important as what you do play. This one uses some eighth notes and changes strings quickly.

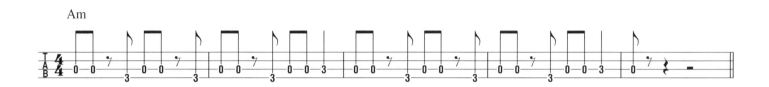

Here's another take based on the rhythmic idea used in that last example. This phrase can be played in an R&B style, but it also works well in rock. You could play this under an E, E7, Em, or Em7 chord. We're moving our hand up to fifth position for this one, which means our first finger is at the fifth fret. Although we could play this riff in open position, we're choosing to play it up in fifth position because the tone is a bit fuller there.

The Counting Crows add life to a basic Am–G5–F progression in "Mr. Jones" by employing rests and mixing in activity with pauses.

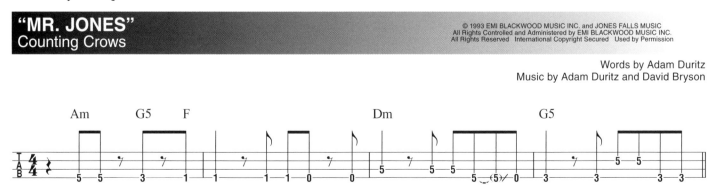

"MR. JONES"
Counting Crows

Words by Adam Duritz
Music by Adam Duritz and David Bryson

The rhythmic hooks are what really make you want to dance when you hear Santana's "Oye Como Va."

"OYE COMO VA"
Santana

Words and Music by
Tito Puente

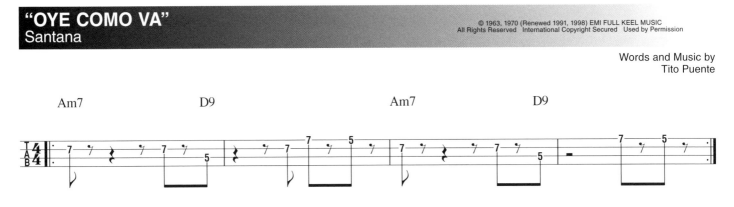

Santana again uses the magic rhythmic formula for his hit, "Smooth," which featured Rob Thomas.

"SMOOTH"
Santana

Words by Rob Thomas
Music by Rob Thomas and Itaal Shur

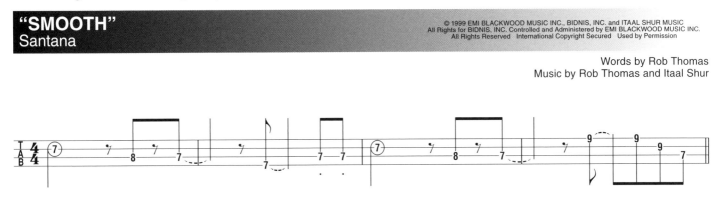

With a strong rhythmic hook, even just two notes can groove harder than anything, as evidenced by Van Halen's "You Really Got Me."

"YOU REALLY GOT ME"
Van Halen

Words and Music by
Ray Davies

Tune down 1 step:
(low to high) $E\flat$–$A\flat$–$G\flat$–$D\flat$

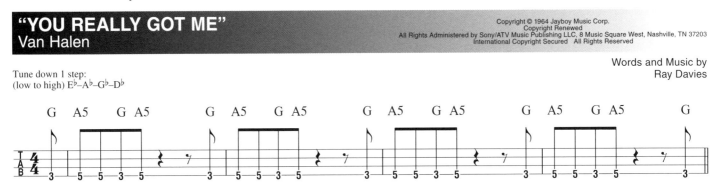

Syncopation

Syncopation is another tool we can use to really groove. To *syncopate* means to place stress on a weak beat, such as an upbeat. That's exactly what we do with this line, which is tailor made for an A7 chord. After the first two A notes, everything else is on the upbeat.

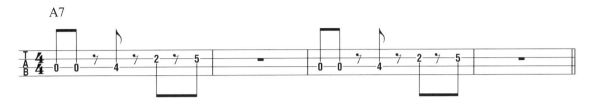

The strong upbeat accents of Cream's "Sunshine of Your Love" give the riff its characteristic groove.

"SUNSHINE OF YOUR LOVE"
Cream

Words and Music by Jack Bruce,
Pete Brown and Eric Clapton

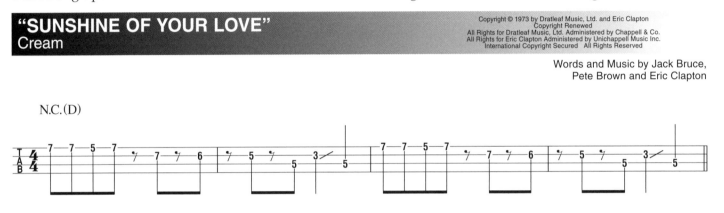

The bass line to Marvin Gaye's classic "What's Going On" uses some tricky upbeat accents. Listen to and play along with the recording.

"WHAT'S GOING ON"
Marvin Gaye

Words and Music by Renaldo Benson,
Alfred Cleveland and Marvin Gaye

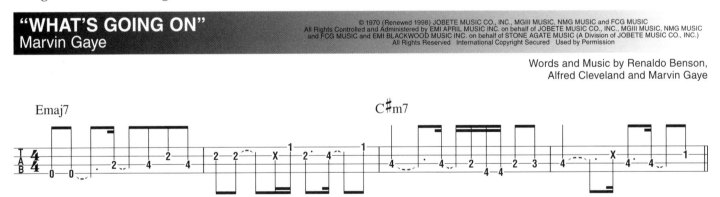

Dead Notes

Another way to really add depth to a groove is to use *dead notes*. This technique is used all the time in busy funk grooves, but it can sound great in an eighth-note line too.

To play a dead note, you release the pressure of your fretting finger so that you're touching the string, but not pressing it down all the way. Watch to DVD to see and hear the difference between playing a note normally, and as a dead note. To get the dead note, we release the pressure with our fretting finger but still maintain contact with the string. This produces a dead-sounding percussive effect that we can add to our bass lines.

Here's an example in the key of E. We're preceding almost every new note with a deadened version of it, played on the eighth note before.

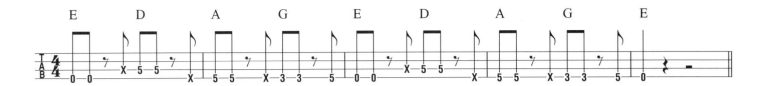

Believe it or not, these little dead notes make quite a difference. Listen to the same thing played without the dead notes to hear for yourself. Sounds quite different, huh? Sometimes the little things can make a big difference in the way something grooves.

The dead notes in Spin Doctors' "Two Princes" are the key to giving the riff its propulsive drive.

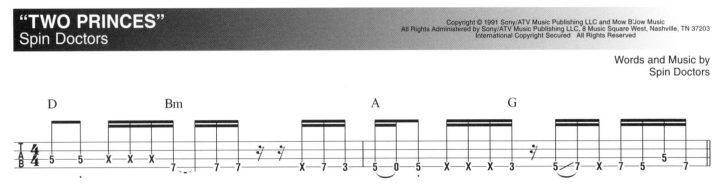

Even on an acoustic number like Oasis' "Wonderwall," the strategic use of dead notes can considerably liven up a bass line.

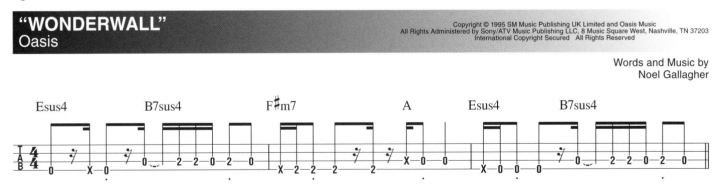

Well, that's gonna do it for this lesson. I hope you enjoyed it and learned some good strategies for coming up with some grooves of your own. Good luck and have fun!